THE
*J*OYFUL
PROFESSOR

How to Shift from Surviving to
T hriving in the Faculty Life

THE
*J*OYFUL
PROFESSOR

How to Shift from Surviving to
*T*hriving in the Faculty Life

Barbara Minsker, Ph.D.

MAVEN
MARK
BOOKS

Published by:
MavenMark Books, LLC
1288 Summit Ave. Suite 107/115
Oconomowoc, WI 53066
www.MavenMarkBooks.com
Please contact the publisher for quantity discounts.

ISBN: 978159598-078-6

Library of Congress Cataloging Number: 2010928130

Cataloging-in-Publication Data:

> Minsker, Barbara.
> The joyful professor : how to shift from surviving to thriving in the faculty
> life / Barbara Minsker.
> p. ; cm.
> Includes bibliographical references.
> ISBN 978-1-59598-078-6
> 1. College teaching--Practice. 2. Work-life balance. 3. Universities and
> colleges--Faculty. 4. College teachers. I. Title.
> LB2332 .M56 2010
> 378.1/2   2010928130

Cover design byEMGraphics.

Printed in the United States of America.

To Brian, Andrew, and Patrick,
my greatest joys.

$\mathcal{A}$ CKNOWLEDGMENTS

$\mathcal{T}$he author thanks the Future Thinking community, who provided such terrific support and ideas for bringing joy to her life, many of which made it into this book. Jan Smith has been a truly wise guide in this journey, and Shannon Jackson Arnold suggested many wonderful resources that are included herein. Sarah Miles contributed several useful time-management tips and the Soulful Values Exercise.

Many colleagues at the University of Illinois contributed to this work, either directly or indirectly. Leslie Srajek contributed to the Life Metaphor Exercise. Pat Sherod and her staff at the Center for Training and Professional Development helped to edit the manuscript and create the Joyful Professor Workshop. The author also thanks her terrific advisors and mentors, especially Vern Snoeyink, Al Valocchi, David Daniel, and Bob Dodds, as well as her immensely talented and hard working students who have been such a joy to work with.

And last, but definitely not least, the author thanks her family. Her parents, Thomas and Aletha Spang, always encouraged her to follow her dreams and to appreciate the joy of learning and discovery. Her husband, Brian Minsker, and children, Andrew and Patrick Minsker, have brought fun to every day and have given such tremendous love and support, even in the face of excessive "AMPing," or being an Absent-Minded Professor.

—Barbara Minsker, Ph.D.

TABLE OF CONTENTS

$\mathscr{P}$REFACE

This is the true joy in life, the being used for
a purpose recognized by yourself as a mighty
one; the being thoroughly worn out before
you are thrown on the scrap heap; the being
a force of Nature instead of a feverish selfish
little clod of ailments and grievances
complaining that the world will not devote
itself to making you happy.
                                    —George Bernard Shaw

$\mathscr{J}$n 1995, I was completing a post-doctoral research associate ("post-doc") position and trying to decide what to do with my life. I had a toddler at home and planned to have another child in the next couple of years. My advisor was encouraging me to apply for faculty positions and I had already been on some interviews, but the lifestyle looked like madness to me. The professors I knew seemed to be constantly running around like chickens with their heads cut off and a number of them were divorced, which could have been related to too many hours in the office, but who knew. I have a strong commitment to my husband and children and wondered if I could possibly be able to find a work-life balance that I could live with.

Nonetheless, the creativity, independence, and adventure of the faculty career was appealing and I couldn't think of another option that was more appealing. So I decided to give it a try and see if I could make it work, and in August 1996 I joined the faculty in environmental engineering and science at the University of Illinois Urbana-Champaign (Illinois). I figured I would put in the time I felt comfortable giving, and if it wasn't enough to make tenure, so be it.

From the start I loved my job: the adventure of pursuing creative ideas that no one had ever tried before and the strong connections I made with students, watching them grow and learn, were so rewarding. I had strong organizational and writing skills, honed by four years of fast-track consulting, but nonetheless my job often felt like "too much of a good thing," a glutton's feast of opportunities and responsibilities that was often overwhelming. In the words of Christopher Robin, I was often a "BISY BACKSON." In A. A. Milne's *The House at Pooh Corner*, Christopher Robin put a note on his door saying: "GONE OUT, BACKSON. BISY, BACKSON," which left the other animals mystified.

By 2007, I had many signs of a successful and balanced life. I had received numerous awards, tenure at a top-tier research institution, and built a strong research, teaching, and service record. I discovered I had a gift for synthesis and building bridges between disparate groups that led to increasing leadership responsibilities in exciting national and campus initiatives. My two sons, one of which was born in my second year at Illinois, were healthy and strong and I made time to connect with them despite a busy travel schedule (35 trips in 2007).

Despite these outer measures of success, I had many internal signs that gave me doubts as to my ability to sustainably continue what I was doing. I loved the challenges and possibilities I could create in large interdisciplinary projects, but the interpersonal issues that came up were building signs of chronic stress overload. I had debilitating migraines that sent me to bed for a day every few months and had regular bouts with allergies and colds. I exercised and did yoga regularly to handle the stress that built up in my body, but still had residual tension that I held in my shoulders, back, and neck. I worried a lot and regularly had "transportation nightmares," in which I could never get my act together to catch my plane, train, or bus.

In summer 2007, I enrolled in leadership courses at the Center for Authentic Leadership (CAL) to try to get some help with the interpersonal aspects of leadership. CAL's Future Thinking program provides an in-depth leadership development community that supports people from all walks of life in finding their true voices and learning communication principles that are the core of both effective leadership and strong relationships.

After enrolling, I learned a tremendous amount about my own strengths and weaknesses, my fundamental needs that I often ignored in taking care of others and the things I "should" be doing, and how to better handle conflicts and connect with others. I've focused on simplifying my life and finding better integration of work and home life, and have made huge progress in reducing stress and transforming from the "BUSI BACKSON" to a truly joyful professor, mother, and spouse.

I have many moments of sheer bliss in my days now, with the promise of more to come. As of this writing, I have gone almost two years without a migraine and my allergies seem to be cured, along with regular transportation nightmares. I'm still learning and growing, but feel I've learned enough to begin to share the results with my colleagues through this guide. What's here is a synthesis of what I've learned over the past 13 years and through my own development work in CAL, but I hope it will be enriched over time by contributions from others who share their ideas and tips.

My intention with this book is to help you to be a productive and successful professor without falling into the "BUSI BACKSON" whirlwind. We'll do this by focusing on the most critical actions to meet your needs, both professional and personal. First we'll identify your most important soulful values and then list some near-term projects and goals that you're interested in. The most critical step for bringing joy to your life will then be in making the key connection from your goals back to your soulful values. This will ensure that your goals will bring you true passion and joy, rather than the endless list of "shoulds" that offer little inspiration. Once we've identified your goals, we'll then examine how to simplify your life to give you time to focus on these essentials, weeding out or delegating the rest. Lastly, we'll summarize some tips for accomplishing your goals and how to avoid common pitfalls that could keep you from meeting them.

Why the focus on goals? Obviously, goals will help you be successful in the academic life, but more importantly, making progress on clear and challenging goals is the fastest path to joy. Mihaly Csikszentmihalyi, in his book *Flow: The Psychology of Optimal Experience*, reports research on thousands of individuals across the world to identify when people most enjoy themselves. The results showed that people were happiest during periods of "flow," when their attention is focused on realistic goals that match their skills. The goals need to be challenging enough for learning and growth to occur, but not so challenging that making progress is impossible. It doesn't matter what the goals are—they could be playing your best soccer game, doing a puzzle with your child, or finding bliss through meditation—as long as they are important to you. Note, though, that it's the process of pursuing the goals that brings joy, not so much the outcome of the process. Too much emphasis on outcomes can lead to stress and disappointment if the goals are not met or have to be changed, which can happen often, particularly when the goals are challenging.

Going through this process of goal setting and focusing will require some upfront time investment, but will pay back huge returns in freeing up your creativity and energy to meet the goals that you care about. In fact, I'm working fewer hours now than I have in the past, but accomplishing more because I'm focusing on the most critical aspects. Keep in mind as you progress through this guide that simplifying and focusing your life is an ongoing process that will evolve over time. In fact, I don't think I'll ever be done with the process, as new challenges are always arising and I am constantly having to make decisions about what activities to keep and what to let go. This guide provides a structure for that continual process to unfold in a constructive way, so don't expect to find an instant fix.

I highly recommend following this book with a small group of collaborators so that you can get help with brainstorming and feedback when you have trouble. As an initial step, work through and discuss the Soulful Values Exercise (page 6) to identify each person's top soulful values. Then follow the Life Metaphor Exercise (page 11) and help each other brainstorm how you might move closer to your ideal vision. Use this information to download and fill out the Goals Template (http://www.joyfulprofessor.com/worksheets.php) and then brainstorm ideas for simplifying your life to meet these goals. Once this setup is complete, re-engage with your group periodically to debrief, following the process outlined on page 48. Throughout your collaboration, follow the guidelines outlined below to create a supportive listening space for your group's interactions.

If you'd like help with this process, please contact me at http://www.joyfulprofessor.com/contact.php about hosting a Joyful Professor Workshop at your campus, or to sign up for one-on-one coaching.

I welcome your questions and feedback on how the process has worked, and any ideas you'd like to contribute to the next version that have worked for you. Contribute to the Joyful Professor discussion by submitting a comment at http://www.joyfulprofessor.com/contact.php. Tell us what works and doesn't work for you, and we'll pass those on.

Barbara Minsker, Ph.D.
Champaign, IL

Barbara Minsker

CREATING A SUPPORTIVE LISTENING SPACE

When working through this book with others, which I highly recommend, create a supportive listening space for each person's growth and insights through the following steps.

- ♦ Commit to making your interactions confidential unless permission is given for sharing outside the group.

- ♦ Ask open-ended questions, which start with "who," "what," "where," "when," or "how," and cannot be answered with "yes" or "no." Avoid using "why."

- ♦ Avoid judging others' situations or offering advice. Remain curious and open-minded, even if you disagree. Reflect back and summarize what you are hearing, but don't try to solve others' problems for them. I've learned the hard way that you can help others far more by walking beside them with deep listening and non-judgmental, open ended questions, than by trying to direct their path through advice.

♦ Speak from your heart, sharing your own experiences using "I" statements.

Chapter One
$\mathscr{S}$ETTING GOALS THAT MEET YOUR NEEDS

In the absence of clearly-defined goals, we become strangely loyal to performing daily trivia until ultimately we become enslaved by it.
　　　　　　　　　　—Robert Heinlein

o find joy in what you do every day, you need to set some goals that are aligned with your own needs (i.e., not just the "shoulds" that you think you should do, but the ones you really want to do). If you're like many professors these days, your life is packed with activity and a never-ending to-do list. To keep from getting sucked into the "BUSI BACKSON" whirlwind, you'll need to be highly intentional about what you take on and disciplined about finding time to meet your needs. To do that, we'll start your goals at a fairly ethereal level and then bring them down to the practical through the following three steps:

STEP 1:
IDENTIFY YOUR TOP SOULFUL VALUES

Developed by Jan Smith, founder of the Center for Authentic Leadership, Figure 1 shows the nine basic Soulful Values that each of us strives to fulfill, whether directly or indirectly.

My top soulful values are:

- Workability/feasibility/efficiency (#5),

- Learning/expanding/curiosity/adventure (#6),

- Making a difference and contributing (#3).

My other key soulful values are:

- ♦   Vitality/sense of aliveness (#8)

- ♦   Playtime/relaxation (#9)

- ♦   Being understood/connected (#2),

My need for learning and adventure has strongly affected the career choices I've made. The learning connection to the professor career is obvious, but I also love to take on high-risk research, teaching, and service activities with "out-of-the-box" approaches rather than more incremental, "safe" choices. My love of the next challenge can threaten my need to be strongly connected with colleagues, friends, and family, though, as challenging activities can require more time and energy and can create stress that leads to shorter tempers.

Living life on the edge of failure is exhilarating, but when something inevitably goes wrong, it can strongly challenge my need for workability and feasibility (leading to my nightmares of missing planes and boarding elevators that never go to the right floor). If the balance among these needs is off, especially if the adventure factor is too low, I get restless, grumpy, and eat too much chocolate and too many cheese puffs. We each have our own set of vices, but to help you be joyful and avoid them, we'll need to keep your top soulful values in mind as we proceed to look at your intentions and goals.

What are your Soulful Values? Ask a friend to help you complete the Soulful Values Exercise on page 6. Then go through and choose three or four of the Soulful Values listed in Figure 1, or portions of the descriptions, that resonate most strongly for you as your "to die for" needs. Take a few moments to ponder the list and see which most appeal to bring into your life more.

Now download and fill out the Soulful Values portion at the top of the goal-setting template available at http://www.joyfulprofessor.com/worksheets.php.

FIGURE 1. COMMON SOULFUL VALUES

Adapted with permission from Jan Smith, Center for Authentic Leadership.

1. **Desire for free choice/freedom/spontaneity**: feeling the freedom to ask questions; say yes or no; having the choice to contribute in a manner that works for you; having the freedom to choose; many options (feeling free, independent, etc.)

2. **Desire for being understood for intentions beneath behaviors**: to feel understood and known is like the lungs' need for air; to be understood about the intent behind behaviors, appearances and words; for one's spirit (feeling connected, known, belonging, and so on)

3. **Desire for making a difference and contributing**: feeling that you are making a meaningful difference and contribution; having a voice; saying what you see; protecting; justice (feeling valued, important and respected)

4. **Desire for giving oneself to a larger whole/vision**: feeling a sense of being connected as an important element of a larger whole; sense of building something important and lasting; feeling of being included and asked for input (feeling included, important and special, and so on)

5. **Desire for workability/feasibility/efficiency**: wanting things to go smoothly, move along and have things be efficient and effective to achieve the desired results (feeling respected, competent, valued, and so on)

6. **Desire for learning/expanding/curiosity/adventure**: naturally loving to grow, learn and discover new possibilities; moving and expanding, trying new things; exploration and adventure; living on the edge of the unknown (feeling of freedom with options, independent, and so on)

7. **Desire for acknowledgment/appreciation for value created**: feeling of being known for the value one creates; for the effort and accomplishments one achieved; for sacrificing oneself on behalf of something (feeling appreciated, known, respected, and fitting in).

8. **Desire for vitality/passion/sense of aliveness/challenge**: feeling energized, passionate and on the edge; having fun; being challenged physically; laughter; at risk (feeling alive and able to cause, and so on)

9. **Desire for playtime, relaxation and "nothing at stake" time**: taking a break from your commitments—work, family obligations and any focused commitments; needing time to stop one's mind from working or intensity (feeling relaxed, cared for, nurtured, and so on)

SOULFUL VALUES EXERCISE

Write down a few things you have done that gave you the most satisfaction or enjoyment, including activities from both your personal and professional life. Be sure to include one or more activities you love to do, regardless of whether or not anyone is watching you or paying you to do them.

Then have your friend ask you open-ended questions to find out what you liked about those activities and help you figure out which of the soulful values listed on page 5 you were filling with that activity. Using only open-ended questions is challenging, but it helps to ensure that the responses you give are truly yours, not your friend's ideas.

When you're the one eliciting responses, a good way to help your friend think more deeply about the things he or she loves to do and explore how it relates to soulful values is to pull phrases from what your friend says and ask what those phrases mean. You'd be surprised how responses often differ from what you might expect! Here are some examples of open-ended questions you could ask someone who loves snow skiing:

- Can you tell me what you love about skiing?
- You mentioned that you prefer to ski on slopes that just push the edge of what you can handle. What does being on "the edge of what you can handle" do for you?
- What comes up in your mind or body when you're in that zone?
- Imagine you're skiing now. What are you noticing that you like the best?
- Can you describe how your five senses engage while you're skiing?
- What makes you want to ski rather than toboggan?
- Whom do you like to ski with, if anyone, and how do you interact with them?

STEP 2:
LIST SPECIFIC, MEASURABLE, ATTAINABLE, REALISTIC, AND TIMELY ("SMART") GOALS.

This step will help you to identify major projects and goals that you most want to accomplish for each project. Before you start, complete the Life Metaphor Exercise on page 11, either alone or with a friend or colleague with whom you can share ideas. This will help you to create an overall vision of your ideal life, or life metaphor, that you want to move toward in your goals.

Continue filling out the Goals Template (available at http://www.joyfulprofessor.com/worksheets.php) with both professional and personal projects. Projects are defined quite broadly, as you can see on the following pages. Pages 8 and 9 show my projects and goals for Spring semester 2010 as an example.

Once you have your projects listed, begin creating specific goals for each one that will help you move toward your ideal life. Typically, goals are for a three- to

---

MY PROJECTS AND GOALS FOR SPRING SEMESTER 2010

<u>My Life Metaphor</u>: A swim in the ocean waves, with a mix of exciting opportunities (jumping through the waves) and relaxation (floating between the waves in the quiet spaces).

I COMMIT TO JUMPING IN THE WAVES BY …

<u>*Intention:*</u>
…learning and growing in leadership adventures, contributing to a larger effort, and connecting with colleagues through:

<u>Soulful value(s) fulfilled with these projects</u>: 3, 6, 2

<u>Project</u>: **Implementing Real-Time Environmental Management Vision**
- Goal: Meet with at least 6 potential research sponsors by 8/31/10
- Goal: Submit three major proposals by 8/31/10
- Goal: Complete IACAT project scoping by 1/31/10

<u>Project</u>: **Sustainability Initiative**
- Goal: Launch education and forum taskforces by 2/15/10
- Goal: Scope themes and launch marketing efforts for each by 2/28/10
- Goal: Prepare and submit journal paper by 8/15/10

<u>Project</u>: **Leadership and Personal Development**
- Goal: Complete daily and weekly structures for new vision
- Goal: Read two books by 5/15/10

<u>*Intention:*</u>
…learning from others and growing, connecting and making a difference to others, and financing adventures through:

<u>Soulful value(s) fulfilled</u>: **6, 3, 2**

<u>Project</u>: **Establish Joyful U, LLC / www.JoyfulU.com**
- Goal: Complete "The Joyful Professor" manuscript by 1/31/10

- Goal: Scope and launch website by 1/31/10
- Goal: Create workshops and disseminate JP marketing materials by 2/28/10

Intention:
… finding adventure, vitality, and rejuvenation n nature through:

Soulful value(s) fulfilled: 6, 8, 9

Project: Outdoor Adventures
- Goal: Planning and going on adventure trips six times / year

I COMMIT TO MAKING QUIET SPACES BETWEEN THE WAVES BY …

Intention:
…connecting with friends and family and enjoying playtime through:

Soulful value(s) fulfilled: 2, 9

Project: Family / Friends
- Goal: Being fully present whenever I am with them
- Goal: Helping to plan at least 2 hours of weekly family time
- Goal: Exploring and acknowledging their world daily

Intention:
… filling my needs for rest, relaxation, and nourishment through:

Soulful value(s) fulfilled: 8

Project: Health
- Goal: Doing aerobic exercise for at least 30 minutes 4 to 5 times/week
- Goal: Eating no more than one sweet serving/week
- Goal: Sleeping at least 7 hours per night

Project: Relaxation, meditation, spirituality
- Goal: Meditating daily and attending church/group weekly
- Goal: Relaxing outside, in the sunshine, or in front of the fire

six-month timeframe, but you can include longer-term goals if you wish.

As you create your goals, try to somehow include the metaphor or words that spoke to you in your ideal vision. For example, I included my ideal vision of life as a swim in the ocean waves, with a mix of exciting opportunities (jumping through the waves) and relaxation (floating in the quiet spaces between the waves). This contrasts with my previous life metaphor, which was swimming in a stormy ocean and being worn out by constant waves. Another participant in my Joyful Life Workshop created a painting of her metaphor showing the four beautiful flowers that she plans to tend, with her four projects listed on each flower.

OTHER TIPS FOR CREATING GOALS.

LIMIT THE NUMBER OF GOALS
Keep the number of goals reasonable so you don't get spread too thin. Include only the projects that are most important to you. Less important projects don't need as careful monitoring and can hopefully be eliminated over

LIFE METAPHOR EXERCISE

Close your eyes and take three deep breaths, quieting your mind. Imagine you are in your favorite place, where you can be most at peace. Look around and feel your five senses engage with the peaceful place. Now think of a metaphor, in words, images, or symbols, that describes your life today.

Now open your eyes and write down what you came up with. Then close your eyes again, go back to your peaceful place, and imagine a metaphor for your perfect life. Open your eyes again and write a paragraph or draw a picture of what you came up with.

Next, brainstorm some ideas for how you can begin to move closer to your ideal vision, or life metaphor.

- What new projects and goals, professional or personal, could you undertake that would start to move you in that direction?

- What might you want to stop doing so that you can find time for this new undertaking? Sometimes a project can involve finding a way to remove yourself from a commitment that is not fulfilling, for example.

Any progress toward your ideal vision, however small, should bring you more joy.

time. As I've become more proficient with this goal-setting process, I find that I have fewer projects listed because I'm slowly weeding out activities that are interesting or enjoyable but are just not as important to me. With a limited number of hours in the day, these have to go to make room for what is most important.

DEVELOP SMART GOALS

Make sure your goals are worded so that you can clearly identify your success within a specified period of time. For example, "Make the world's environment sustainable" is definitely not specific enough or measurable, and it's certainly not realistic or attainable for a short-term goal. Identify a more specific first step that you would take to move toward such a long-term vision, such as "Create and teach a course on environmental sustainability by November 30, 2010."

STRETCH YOURSELF

Don't be afraid to stretch yourself and to get wild with your goals. You only live once, and "maybe someday" is a good way to let life pass you by. If you have a long-term vision that you've been putting off for a while, identify a short-term goal toward that vision and add it to your list, even if you can't imagine finding the time to do it now. Your goals need to be ones you find exciting, not the "shoulds." We'll deal with the unexciting "shoulds" later.

One of the participants in a Joyful Professor workshop loved her job teaching at a Midwestern college, but her heart yearned for the pulse of a more urban environment. She decided to approach a colleague in New York City to arrange to spend summers in a more metropolitan location, which would still allow her to keep the academic job she loved and satisfy her yen for the cosmopolitan lifestyle.

TAKE YOUR TIME
While change can be great, it can also be scary, so don't feel you have to radically transform your life overnight. Sometimes you may feel like you took two steps forward and one step back from your ideal vision, but keep following your heart towards a life that better meets your needs.

Barbara Minsker

MAINTAIN A GROWTH MINDSET

Keep yourself in a "growth mindset" in setting and pursuing your goals. In her book *Mindset: The New Psychology of Success*, Carol Dweck summarizes her research on fixed and growth mindsets. People who are living in a fixed mindset believe their intelligence and talents are fixed and cannot be changed much through their efforts, while living in a growth mindset means you believe anything can be substantially changed through effort and experience.

Living in a growth mindset means that you take on new challenges as an opportunity to learn and grow from the mistakes you make along the way. Living in a fixed mindset leads to striving towards appearances (e.g., making yourself look smart by avoiding difficult challenges, trying to cover up mistakes, and avoiding feedback) and outcomes (e.g., focusing on awards) to show the world that you really are smart, even if you don't believe it yourself (often referred to as the "imposter syndrome").

Dweck's research has shown that the most successful people have a growth mindset, and that anyone can learn to live in a growth mindset. However we are often trained into a fixed mindset through early emphasis on achievements rather than growth. I now believe that much of the stress I've experienced has been due to living in a fixed mindset, leading to a terrible fear of failure despite numerous successes. I'm working toward living in a growth mindset, and the reduction in stress levels from that alone has been amazing. If you struggle with any of these issues, I highly recommend Dweck's book.

For professional goals, ideally you want to identify goals that both meet your needs and produce outcomes that your institution values highly (publications, grants, awards, good teaching evaluations, etc.). If you're new to the professor gig, see tips for identifying outcomes that your institution values in the Appendix. If you can't think of any goals you're interested in that your institution will value, perhaps it's time to consider retirement or a new career, which could easily be listed as a personal goal.

STEP 3: IDENTIFY YOUR INTENTIONS FOR EACH GOAL.

Map your goals to the needs you identified in Step 1 by writing down your higher intentions for each goal. Higher intentions state how each goal will meet one or more of the Soulful Values you identified earlier. They should reflect what you are trying to accomplish with the goal, the "why" you want to meet the goal to fill your soulful values, rather than the specific way you will go about meeting that need. Refer to the Soulful Values listed on page 5 for general ideas of intentions listed under each soulful value. I have given specific examples on my own list of goals on pages 8 and 9, where I grouped my projects and goals under a set of intentions that cover my "to-die-for" needs.

Now, write out the soulful values listed on page 5 that are met by that intention. If you find that one of your goals doesn't contribute to any of your top needs, reconsider whether you want to pursue that goal or not. Likewise, if one of your top needs doesn't map to any of your goals, reconsider whether that need is important to you and, if it is, come up with a goal to fulfill it.

Thinking about goals in this way is challenging at first and takes some practice, but the exercise can be incredibly illuminating for identifying where you most want to spend your time. After making my list, I realized why I've always had more trouble getting motivated about completing existing research projects rather than going after new ones, as there is far less adventure in an existing project than in new possibilities. Because of this, I ask my students and employees to take major responsibilities on current projects so I can free up time for more adventurous pursuits. I used to feel guilty about doing this, but now that I understand "why," I give myself the grace to follow my heart. It also allows my students and post-docs more freedom to learn and grow than they would if I were supervising them more closely.

This step will probably be the most challenging one for most people who have never thought about their underlying intentions before, but it is also the most important step to becoming a joyful professor, creating a more joyful YOU, rather than someone who is going through the motions because of the "shoulds." Take the time to think through this step, and write down your intentions for each goal. If you make a habit of doing this, you'll find that the intentions bring your goals to life, helping you to remember why you wanted to accomplish that goal in the first place.

Now that you've captured your high-level goals on paper, you'll want to put the first tasks needed for accomplishing your goals on your to-do list. But first, let's simplify your life, including your to-do list, so that you can find more time to focus on what you really want to accomplish.

Chapter Two

SIMPLIFYING AND
FOCUSING YOUR LIFE

Learning to live in the present moment is part of the path of joy.
—Sarah Ban Breathnach

The professor's life is filled with numerous time demands and it's easy to lose focus and become overwhelmed when the "to do" list stretches a mile long and keeps growing. Good time management will free your mind up from thinking about the minutiae and keep you focused on the important things. Here are some guidelines for simplifying and finding focus:

SIMPLIFY YOUR COMMITMENTS.

As you go through your day, think about how you're spending your time. Which activities are taking up the most time? Identify the tasks that only you can do and ask other people if they can do the other tasks or eliminate them.

Draw on any help you have available (research assistants, administrative assistants, teaching assistants, graders, and any other colleagues available to you) as partners in your goals. Your graduate students can benefit from learning how to write grant proposals or teach classes and you can benefit from spending less time on those tasks. Even minor tasks can add up to take a large chunk out of your day and detract from meeting your goals, so don't ignore the pile-up of minutiae.

When you ask others to take on tasks, give them as much creative problem solving and decision making authority as possible so you can spend your time on the tasks that you really need to do. This will make the task more interesting and rewarding for them, as well as allowing you to spend time on your goals. If you're going to micro-manage, you might as well do it yourself because it will take less time. Focus on meeting your higher intentions, not particular steps for carrying them out, and accept that the tasks may not be done quite the way you would. Remember that you're freeing up time to meet your goals, especially those personal goals that you may have been putting off for "someday".

If you have a goal in mind that would make a major contribution to your institution, ask for reduced assignments or extra help to achieve it. For example, for three years when I led the development of the proposed WATERS Network, I only taught one course and had reduced university service commitments. When I was a new professor, I received extra teaching assistant and grader help when I was overwhelmed. Don't be afraid to ask. If your institution has few resources or help available, you can even consider outsourcing some of your tasks through a service. See *The 4-Hour Work Week* by Timothy Ferriss for ideas and resources on outsourcing, which can cost as little as $5/hour.

CREATE FOCUSED TO–DO LISTS.

Whether you use computer software or old-fashioned pen and paper, split your tasks into the following three lists. Don't keep a list? You have an amazing memory, but you can put your brain power to better use by writing down your tasks and freeing up that mental power for more creative functions.

Goal Tasks: This is where you list the specific tasks you want to accomplish to move toward the goals you laid out. For example, writing the chapters of this book went on my "Goal Tasks" list. Mark the tasks that are most likely to give you the greatest progress toward your goal, or that have firm deadlines, as high priority. Set aside time every day to accomplish at least a few of these tasks, and you'll feel great when you check them off and know you're making substantial progress on your goals.

Non-Goal Tasks: This is where you list all the other myriad demands that don't meet your goals. This is the list where I put writing progress reports, minor committee work, cleaning my office, and the plethora of other minutiae that don't contribute to one of my goals. Think carefully before you add anything to this list: Is it really essential? Can someone else do it? Will there be a negative consequence if you don't do it, or do it later?

Future Tasks: These are tasks that you'll need to do in the future, but can't or don't need to do now. Tasks here could be reminders to follow up on requests that haven't been filled (e.g., finalizing a meeting time after you hear from the other participants) or things you'll need to do that depend on your or someone else's action first (e.g., editing a conference paper that your student is drafting). This list could also include tasks that you'd like to do someday, but there are no real consequences if you never get to them (e.g., "cleaning my office" was on my "Future Tasks" list for some time).

If these tasks are important to you, schedule time for them during quiet periods in your life. If they sit on your list undone for a few years, perhaps they're not too important and could be removed. Getting these future tasks in a list keeps them from cluttering up your head (reducing focus) and provides peace of mind that you'll remember to follow up if needed to keep your goals moving. For example, a task on this list to schedule a meeting could remind you to follow up with someone who has been recalcitrant at giving you available times.

As you add tasks to these lists, be sure they are:

- *Specific and broken into small enough pieces* so that you can accomplish them within a reasonable period of time (a few hours, and certainly no more than a day). For each goal you created, add the smallest first steps to your list individually. Vague, giant tasks will sit like a rock on your list and never get done. For example, rather than adding a task to my "Goal Tasks" list to write this entire book, I made individual tasks for each chapter and only put one chapter on the list at a time. Add follow-on tasks to your "Future Tasks" list if you need help remembering the next steps after your initial tasks.

- *Things that you personally must do and can't ask others to do*. Is this task essential for you personally to do? If not, can someone else do it? For example, I've stopped reading the literature in my field because my students and post-docs summarize the pertinent literature related to their work for me, and they help me with checking literature reviews in paper or proposal reviews. This frees up time for me to get creative research ideas from other sources (e.g., talking with colleagues in other fields), since I find that my best research ideas come from outside my field. My students and post-docs help with researching other fields once a promising idea is identified, and I also strongly encourage them to get creative and generate new ideas themselves.

USE YOUR CALENDAR WISELY.

Whether you use a paper or computer-based calendar to keep track of appointments, be sure to:

♦ *Identify your most productive working time* (morning for me) and schedule large chunks of this time for focused progress on the most creative and time-consuming tasks needed to achieve your goals (e.g., writing). Schedule this time on your calendar and hold yourself to it at least a few days a week.

Avoid scheduling meetings during your most productive working time whenever possible and block that time off on your calendar. Put off interruptions and find a quiet place where you can really make progress. I know colleagues who hide in the library or coffee shops, or work at home (my strategy), so they can have uninterrupted creative working time. Keep the e-mail closed, the phone unplugged, and the door closed.

Schedule meetings in your less productive times (afternoons for me) and put off requests during your most productive hours whenever possible. If your less productive time is full, will there be any harm in delaying the meeting until you have an open time? If not, ask for a later date. If you find that productive working time is continually getting eaten up with meetings, it may be a sign that you are doing too much. Are there any commitments you can delegate or eliminate? Remember, even small ones can distract from your goals and add up to a large chunk of time, especially if they involve meetings.

As much as possible, squeeze less time-consuming tasks and minutiae into the times when you can't tackle the time-consuming creative tasks (between meetings, late in the day, etc.). Discipline yourself not to procrastinate on the time-consuming tasks by working on lots of small tasks during your peak work periods (splitting your big tasks into smaller pieces can help with this). E-mail is a common distracter in this way (more on this in a moment). If you do need to take more time for the minutiae than you can squeeze in during odd times, try batching a number of small tasks together, which is much more efficient than continually interrupting your productive work time with these distractions.

If you have to schedule a lot of meetings and don't have an administrative assistant who can handle it for you, consider using a calendar system that will allow you to make the calendar available to others on the Web. That way, they can propose specific meeting times to you and you don't have to spend time typing all the times you're available in an e-mail (a major bane of my existence in the past). For scheduling large group meetings, online meeting schedulers like Doodle are so much easier than sifting through endless e-mails with everyone's availability.

Also, be sure to set alarms for important appointments so you don't miss them. Once you find the "flow" on your goal tasks, you may forget what time it is!

TAME THE E-MAIL DEMON.

These days, e-mail can so easily take over your life. Once I began leading major projects with numerous collaborators, I was easily getting 70-100 e-mail messages a day. Sometimes, I felt like I could sit at my desk all day and just do e-mail. After a particularly busy period over several months, my e-mails had piled up to 600 messages in my inbox. I then took the drastic step of deleting the 500 oldest messages, figuring if it was important enough, they'd e-mail me again. Having reached this crisis level, I've finally found a system that got the e-mail under control, which is adapted from a posting in www.unclutterer.com and tips in *The 4-Hour Work Week*:

♦ *Limit your e-mail time*: Whenever possible, turn off the auto-checker on your e-mail (or shut your e-mail program) and download and respond to e-mails only once or twice a day. If you are expecting something more urgent and have to check e-mail in between, skim the subject titles to look for the message you need, but don't be tempted to deal with anything else. Avoid skimming message titles whenever possible, since the temptation to look at the other messages will be strong.

♦   If you're concerned that you'll miss something important, you can put an *auto-reply* on your e-mail account giving a phone number to reach you in emergencies (a cell phone, perhaps), put your policy in the signature of your e-mails and list an emergency phone number, or just mention your policy to those that you work closest with so they know to call you when it's urgent. Explain that you're trying to create space in your life for creative work that requires uninterrupted time.

♦   *Unsubscribe* from newsletters and listservs that don't meet your goals. There are many newsletters and listservs that will bombard you with messages, clog your inbox, and distract you from your goals via information overload. Think about how much value you're getting from each one and unsubscribe from all but the few that are most valuable to your personal and professional goals. You can also ask your students or post-docs to send you the most relevant news that you shouldn't miss.

◆ *Set up a simple folder system* for organizing e-mails. I used to have a complicated set of folders for storing e-mails related to every project, class, proposal, etc. Each message had to be stored in the right folder, which took extra time, and the system became so complex that I often couldn't find messages by browsing later anyway. E-mail search engines are powerful and fast enough these days that it's better to take advantage of them and use a very simple and fast filing system. Below are the four folders I use now, and the next bullet discusses how to use them effectively.

  – <u>Follow Up</u>: This folder stores the messages that I need to respond to later, or take some other action to deal with them (e.g., a draft paper to review). Remove these messages after you respond or complete the action.

  – <u>Hold</u>: This folder stores messages that I will need to access in the next few days and want to keep handy (e.g., comments on a document that colleagues have sent me and I will be revising shortly or directions to an upcoming event). Clean this folder out periodically.

– Archive: This folder stores messages that I'm done with but want to keep. At the end of the year you can add a year to the title and start a new "Archive" folder if you want to keep the folder from getting too massive over the years.

– Bacon: Some messages have useful value (e.g., an interesting article someone sent you) and take more than two minutes to read, but are not worth putting on your to-do list. This folder is a repository for such messages, which have more nutritional content than spam and can be read when you have a quiet time to do so. Be sure not to put any time-critical items here though, since they may sit for quite a while.

♦ Deal with every e-mail immediately after you read it: When you sit down to read your messages, deal with each one immediately: If a message requires reading or a response that will take less than two minutes, read or respond immediately and delete the message, or move it to your Archive or Hold folder. If the message requires more time, add it to the appropriate to-do list and put it in the Follow-Up folder. Take a second to think about whether the task is really necessary, particularly if it's not contributing to any of your goals. If the message contains useful information but is not important enough to clutter your to-do list, put it in the Bacon folder.

If you don't have time to deal with each message immediately, don't bother checking your e-mail as you'll waste time reading messages twice.

If you follow this e-mail system diligently, you'll be amazed how much time will be freed up to focus on the activities you care about.

DON'T MULTI-TASK.

I never, ever thought I would write those words, as I was once the master multi-tasker—typing e-mails during meetings, working through meals, thinking about other problems when someone was talking to me, and so on.

My family has an acronym for the result of my mental multi-tasking: AMP (Absent-Minded Professor, as in "Mom's AMPing again…"). I still catch myself doing it occasionally but I always regret it, because it leads to poor focus, lost time because things that I missed have to be repeated, and a lack of connection with others. If something is important enough for you to spend time on it, give it your full attention. Be fully in the moment, focused on the task and, if you're interacting with someone, be fully engaged with them and open and curious about what they have to say.

If something is not important enough for you to give it your full time and attention, consider removing yourself from the meeting or eliminating the task, since you're probably not contributing much if you're multi-tasking. Will there be any serious long-term impacts if you do? If not, simplify your life and get rid of it.

One of my biggest challenges with multi-tasking is clearing my head of all the thoughts running through it. I like to take on challenging projects and live my life a bit on the edge of what I can handle (my need for adventure again), which means that things I need to remember to do are constantly popping up and distracting me from what's at hand. If this happens to you too, carry a small notebook with you at all times and immediately write down your idea or a task that needs to go on your to-do list to get it out of your head. Later you can transfer it to your to do list or take care of it immediately if it's a small task.

If you're still having trouble focusing, consider taking a meditation or yoga class to learn how to clear your head of all your thoughts and worries and just be. When you learn to live in the moment, no matter how mundane the task, the world suddenly becomes an amazing place with so much more joy.

Last fall, I took a meditation class and have been practicing daily. Meditation helps to clear my mind and reduce anxiety about the past or future, be more compassionate toward myself and others, and stay focused on the present. *Wherever You Go There You Are: Mindfulness Meditation in Everyday Life*, by Jon Kabat-Zinn is a very useful guide for getting started. I highly recommend taking a class or retreat as well, which can help support regular practice and give answers to your questions. The

Insight Meditation Society has an extensive list of resources and retreats at http://dharma.org/ims/ss_meditation_resources.htm.

I also highly recommend reading *A New Earth: Awakening to Your Life's Purpose* for more on living in the moment. In it, author Eckhart Tolle recommends taking on your activities in one of three modes:

♦ *Acceptance*: This is for the tasks that you don't want to do (your "Non-Goal Tasks" list), but know you need to do. If you can't accept that you need to do it and it brings you continued frustration, try to find a creative way to get it off your plate. I was constantly frustrated with the amount of time I was spending typing out available meeting times in e-mails, so I switched to a calendar system that would allow public posting. This dramatically reduced the amount of time I spend on e-mail.

   If you can't eliminate the task, you may want to put it off as long as you can (sometimes tasks will go away if you wait long enough, or maybe you'll come up with an idea for delegating it, or at least the task will be more exciting if it's last minute). When you must do the task, accept that you need to do it and focus on getting it done as quickly and efficiently as possible so you can move on to other things. Stay in the moment as you're doing even these tasks, though, and you may find some surprising joy in the most mundane tasks. I recently rediscovered my love of water play in doing the dishes that makes even this routine duty much more fun.

♦ *Enjoyment*: This is for the activities that you love to do just for sheer fun, with no purpose in mind. You would do these activities even if no one was watching you and you weren't getting any rewards for them. Make sure your personal goals lead to some of these activities on your list, and try to intersperse them in your day in small doses to recharge yourself. Try the Enjoyment Exercise on the opposite page if you have trouble figuring out what activities would bring you more enjoyment.

♦ *Enthusiasm.* This last mode is for the things that you enjoy doing and that have a higher purpose. The tasks that you enjoy and will meet your higher intentions and soulful values fall into this category, and they should bring you great satisfaction to

ENJOYMENT EXERCISE

If you've been so focused on doing what you "should" do for many years, you may initially have trouble coming up with activities that you can do just for sheer enjoyment. Think back to times in your life when you were less busy and what you loved to do then. What was it about those activities that led you to enjoy them?

If you can figure out what you enjoyed about these activities, you can find ways of injecting those aspects into your day. I've always loved being out in nature and used to think that I could only get that joy through trips to beautiful places (Central Illinois not being well known for its beauty). Only recently I discovered (with help from Jan Smith and her amazing advanced leadership course, Future Thinking) that I love to watch and hear movement in nature (water flowing, branches swaying, birds flying, clouds and light changes) and I realized that I can find the same joy by taking a few moments to fully focus my attention out my office window at a single tree or the sky. Now I've got enjoyment on tap wherever I go and can find a few birds or a tree to look at for a few moments.

Another way I've found for squeezing in enjoyment is to find something fun or beautiful to look at wherever I go, whether it's a whimsical decoration on a wall or a beautiful flower. This works especially well when standing around waiting in lines. I can't tell you what a difference these small steps have made! Take a few moments to notice what's around you and draw enjoyment out of it.

complete. For example, writing this guide is a task that I have done with enthusiasm. I had never tried to write a non-technical work and had great fun playing with the words in a much less structured format than technical papers. You should have plenty of tasks on your list that you will be able to complete in this mode after our goal-setting exercise.

TAKE CARE OF YOURSELF.

I can't emphasize this one enough. If you burn the candle at both ends trying to get things done, you may get away with it for a while, sometimes even years, but eventually it will catch up with you in the form of physical or mental illness. You'll also be much less focused and productive when you work if you haven't been taking care of yourself.

Don't try to work for long hours straight without taking some sort of mental or physical break that will recharge your batteries and keep you working efficiently. Pick whatever type of break recharges you best. For me, it's exercise outside, yoga, or recently, meditation. I find when I take a walk or do yoga around lunchtime, I get more of my goals done overall because I'm able to focus better in the afternoon and not just resort to mindless tasks or endless meetings in which I can't focus because I'm too burned out. I've also been experimenting with interspersing work and play a lot more and am finding that I'm much more creative and alert all day long. I'm working fewer hours and getting more quality work done, and stress just doesn't build up any more. Inspiration is just as likely (and probably more likely) to come while you're taking a walk than sitting in your office.

You'll see in my personal goals on pages 8 and 9 that I have several related to taking care of myself, because I have a bad habit of not doing so and I always regret it later. Going through pregnancy, childbirth, and raising two young boys while trying to get tenure, my needs usually came last. Over the years, I've learned that if I don't get enough sleep and exercise, at best I am unable to focus and be as productive during my work times and I'm grumpy at home, and at worst I get colds, allergy flare-ups, and migraines. I know others who have slid into serious depression and major mid- and late-life crises because they ignored their needs for so many years.

Figure out what you need to function well, add that to your personal goals, and make sure you find a way to arrange your life to meet them. Don't feel guilty about the time it takes to take care of yourself, as you'll be a much better worker and parent/spouse/partner/friend during the other times. If you find you've been so overloaded that you're not meeting your basic personal needs for an extended period, re-assess your commitments and offload some tasks until you can get back to a sustainable level.

If you're pregnant or have a baby in the house and meeting your sleep needs is impossible, schedule naps in your calendar so you can stay as alert as possible all day. When I was pregnant with my second child, I scheduled one-hour naps every day after lunch. That gave me enough time to get to the nap location and settle in (a locker room with a couch that was rarely used), fall asleep, and still get forty minutes or so of sleep to recharge. I kept an alarm clock, small pillow, and a blanket in my office during that period. The productivity gains I experienced during the rest of the day far outweighed the extra time it took.

Even if you're sleeping well at night, closing your eyes and resting in your office for 15 minutes can make a big difference in your ability to function at a high level. I've bought a comfortable chair and footrest for my office that I use for spot naps when needed, an investment that keeps me productive (and joyful!) the rest of the day. If you don't have a private office, try to find a place where you can recharge in peace for a few minutes—perhaps a comfortable chair or couch in a quieter place in your building, a bench outside, or your car.

Chapter Three

$\mathscr{G}$ ETTING YOUR GOALS DONE

*Things won are done;
joy's soul lies in the doing.*
—William Shakespeare, *Troilus and
Cressida, Act 1, Scene 2*

$\mathcal{W}$e covered some of the tips that will help you get your goals done in the previous section, but let's put it all together in some simple guidelines:

FOCUS, FOCUS, FOCUS...

When you start work during your most productive work time, jump right in and work on your highest priority tasks that require the most creativity, ideally the tasks that will advance your goals the most. Work in a quiet place where you can keep e-mail, phone, and other people at bay until other, less productive times in the day. Put other issues out of your mind and focus on engaging all of your creative energy into the task at hand.

ASSESS AND BALANCE THE TRADEOFFS.

On any given day, you will probably have more tasks demanding your attention than you will possibly be able to accomplish. Some may be non-goal tasks with pressing deadlines that will need your immediate attention. Give non-goal tasks attention when you must, but if they are consistently preventing you from taking on goal tasks during your productive work period, go back to the guidelines in the previous section and re-evaluate. See if you can find a way to reduce your commitments, ask others to take on tasks, or eliminate tasks if there are no significant consequences. Even minor tasks can be a major drain on your energy when they distract you from focusing on your goals: every time you have to re-start a creative task, it takes extra time and energy to re-focus on it.

In balancing tradeoffs among tasks, also consider long-term efficiency in getting to your ultimate goal. If you have colleagues or students who are helping achieve the goal, they may need an upfront investment of your time to get them started (e.g., holding a meeting to discuss the approach or creating an outline with writing assignments). This task may be higher priority than a task that only requires your attention, such as writing your own section of the paper, since it will allow your collaborators to work in parallel with you. Identify the "critical path" to getting your goal done in the time desired, and give tasks on that critical path your highest priority.

BATCH THE DISTRACTIONS.

When you can't eliminate the distractions, batch them into periods when you are least productive on major tasks (I call this "batching the bullshit"). I try to schedule all my meetings in the afternoon so I can have quiet work time in the mornings when I'm most productive. I try to put off morning meetings for anything but emergencies so that I can keep focused. During gaps between meetings or at the end of the day, I batch the minutiae like scheduling meetings, making quick phone calls, or doing e-mails.

REWARD YOURSELF.

Make a promise to reward yourself in a concrete way for progress you make towards your goals, especially if you find yourself procrastinating on major tasks, even after breaking them into smaller pieces. Find a healthy indulgence like one of your activities that you do for sheer enjoyment. I often reward myself with reading a juicy novel on the back deck in summer or in front of a cozy fire in winter. Don't be afraid to pamper yourself like this on a regular basis; it will help you to focus and be fully present when you need to, whether it's on work or family and friends.

BE FLEXIBLE IN YOUR GOALS AND TASKS, BUT NOT YOUR INTENTIONS.

No matter what you do, circumstances will change and you may find that your original goal is no longer desirable or appropriate, or needs modification. The research project that sounded so interesting may turn out to be a dead end, or the teaching method you tried out may flop. When that happens, go back to your goal sheet and adjust as needed. Get creative and find new ways to meet your higher intentions and needs. Always be flexible in how you carry out your intentions, but never give up on meeting your needs somehow.

DEBRIEF YOUR PROGRESS ON A REGULAR BASIS.

Periodically revisit and debrief on your goals, intentions, and tasks. You'll need to update your goals and intentions every few months or so to keep yourself focused. I revise mine at the beginning of each semester and the summer, which seems about right for me. Also review your goals, to-do list, and calendar on a weekly or bi-weekly basis to see what might need adjustment. Do you need to add some new tasks to push your goals along? Are you not spending enough time on an important goal? Scheduling time for it on your calendar is a must. Are you spending too much time on non-goal activities? See if you can ask others to do them, or put them off to a later time.

In addition to revisiting the goals yourself, find a friend or colleague with whom you can debrief your progress on a regular basis. Share your goals and intentions with that person and discuss what's working and what isn't. Follow these debriefing steps from the Center for Authentic Leadership. You can download a Debriefing Exercise template from http://www.joyful-professor.com/worksheets.php to help with implementing these steps for each of your projects:

♦ Is there a communication breakdown in your activities that is preventing or delaying progress? For example, do you know how to make requests in a partnership way, where mutual expectations, timelines, and commitments are clearly defined for everyone involved? Are there some new skills you could learn that would help, and where might you find help with that?

Again, I highly recommend the CAL leadership development program at http://www.authentic-

leadership.com, which provides in-depth guidance
and practice for effective communication skills.

♦   Are there structures, processes, methods, or recurring
    items (e.g., recurring appointments or tasks that
    would help you make regular progress) that are
    missing? What structures or skills are leading to your
    successes? Can you identify new structures or
    processes that might help you to improve progress on
    goals that aren't working as you had hoped?

    For example, maybe you need the structure of a
    regular meeting with your mentor or a colleague to
    discuss how things are going and what directions to
    take in the future. Or you might just need to set
    alarms on your calendar to remind you to focus on a
    goal task at a particular time.

♦   Are there mindsets that work or don't work for you?
    For example, I used to have a fixed mindset that I
    should be working all the time, either on my job or
    on home obligations. This mindset meant that I felt
    guilty about taking care of my own needs, which
    made me tired and grumpy by the end of the day.
    Now I've shifted to a growth mindset, where I'm
    learning new ways to take care of my needs while

keeping my commitments to a level that I can handle. Maintaining a joyful life balance is now a growth challenge that I relish.

Having a trusted friend or colleague to help you brainstorm ideas and provide support when you're struggling is incredibly useful. For example, I had a "triad" of two other participants in the Future Thinking program whom I talked with weekly.

With this basic framework in mind, let's now look at each of the areas where professors typically spend their time and point out some tips and pitfalls.

Chapter Four

$\mathcal{T}$HRIVING AS A PROFESSOR

*It must be borne in mind that the tragedy in
life doesn't lie in not reaching your goal.
The tragedy lies in having no goal to reach.
It isn't a calamity to die with dreams
unfulfilled, but it is a calamity not to
dream... Not failure, but low aim is sin.*
—Benjamin E. Mays

$\mathcal{N}$ow let's look in more detail at some of the challenges facing professors in balancing the myriad of demands on their time. We'll start with research goals and then move on to teaching, service, and personal goals.

RESEARCH GOALS.

For most professors in science and engineering fields, the research cycle involves finding funding, managing projects, and publishing research results. Since these are the steps I know best, I will focus on those. Professors who don't chase funding should still find some helpful tips in the other two sections.

FINDING FUNDING

Focus is critical here. Identify the most promising sources of funding by talking with colleagues in your field or your former advisor if you're just starting out. Visit the potential funders personally to discuss your ideas so you can craft a proposal most relevant to your common interests with the sponsor. Maintain a good relationship with sponsors over time through periodic visits or phone calls, or by helping them out with workshops or proposal reviews. Having a personal relationship with the research sponsor can make the difference between a strong proposal that is funded and one that is not, particularly in today's competitive research environment where there are often far more strong proposals than funds available.

In selecting proposal topics, build from your strengths. If you have to do a lot of background reading in an area to write a credible proposal, you're not working in an area of strength. If you've been in the faculty game for a while and want to launch a new research focus, realize that it will probably take years of investment (either from investing your own time or, if you're lucky, investing exploratory research funds or a fellowship student's time) to build enough of a base in a new area to be competitive in national proposal competitions. I've changed research focus several times because I invariably get bored staying in the same area too long (my need for adventure again), but I've been fortunate to be able to get exploratory research funds from my university to grease the skids.

In writing proposals, don't be afraid to ask your students or post-docs to help out or even take the lead on preparing and submitting the proposal. They will learn a valuable skill that will be useful regardless of where they end up, and you will benefit from freeing up more time.

MANAGING PROJECTS

Once you've got a research project, you'll probably need to work with other people to get the research done, whether it's research assistants, post-docs, collaborating professors, administrative assistants, or all of the above. Sometimes this can be a joy and sometimes it can be a major source of stress. If you're leading large projects, consider taking a good leadership course to learn how to build strong partnerships for making progress on a common vision (I highly recommend the Center for Authentic Leadership's courses, which have literally been life-changing for me and many others). Always remember your higher intentions and be flexible about how the project is carried out. Here are some brief tips to help smooth the process:

♦ *Coordinating responsibilities*
   Particularly if you are leading a large project, you'll need to ask others to do as much of the work as possible. Don't underestimate the amount of time it will take you to coordinate all of the tasks and personnel and leave your time open to step in when help is needed. For example, I led a group creating a

national vision document for the WATERS Network and initially, assigned all of the sections to other authors. When one of the authors was unable to complete his assignment, I was able to write major sections of the chapter because I wasn't working on other sections.

♦ *Productive meetings and conference calls*
Schedule meetings only when you really need them, not just for the sake of routine. I recently eliminated all routine meetings with my students, staff, and post-docs, following the recommendations of Cali Ressler and Jody Thompson's book *Why Work Sucks and How to Fix It: No Meetings, No Joke — The Simple Change that Can Make Your Job Terrific.*

To make this approach feasible, I ask each person to first create a set of short-term and long-term goals for the work. Once we agree upon the goals, team members periodically e-mail me updates on their progress, any difficulties they've encountered, and whether they need to meet with me or others about a particular issue. This focuses our discussions on the work that needs to be done and has freed up a tremendous amount of time on my calendar that I can use to address the real needs as they come up.

When you do have a meeting, prepare (or better yet have someone else prepare) an agenda or talking points and go through them quickly and efficiently, politely interrupting when conversation gets off track. Summarize conclusions as you go, making sure everyone agrees with them, and assign action items for follow ups after the meeting. Assign someone to send out a written summary of the conclusions and action items, and follow up with reminders as needed for critical action items that are important to meeting your goals.

♦ *Working with busy people*
These days, most everyone seems to operate with very full plates and invariably, some tasks won't get done on time or at all. Make a note on your "future tasks" to-do list to periodically follow up with those who have critical assignments on which the project's success hinges and see if they are making progress and have encountered any problems.

Particularly with time-critical projects, encourage the project participants to tell you about problems they're encountering sooner rather than later, so you can work with them to find a solution. Avoid getting judgmental about their problem (you have no idea what's going on in their life) and just ask open-ended questions ("Tell me more about that..", "What's happening with…", "How do you see this…") so you can understand what caused the problem and help brainstorm a solution.

At times you may encounter people who are so busy that they are completely nonresponsive to your requests or follow-ups. Don't assume that a non-response means that there are no problems, because more often than not, they are wrapped up in other tasks and not even thinking about your project. Keep sending e-mails or leaving messages every couple of days. If they're still not responsive or you need a quicker answer, keep calling without leaving messages until you catch them. Be patient and understanding about what they are dealing with, but persistent about finding a solution that will work for both of you. Remember to focus on meeting your higher intentions, not necessarily any particular path to do so.

HANDLING CONFLICTS

Particularly if you're managing a large project, invariably there will be conflicts that arise among the team members. Avoid making judgments about people's intelligence or commitment, since you will never know the whole story of what they are dealing with. Instead, get curious and ask open-ended questions that allow others to tell you their stories without leading them to your conjectures. Once you understand all the facts from all the relevant parties, try to identify and articulate their higher intentions (from Figure 1 on page 5) and see if you can creatively brainstorm a solution to the conflict that still meets their (and your!) higher intentions. Be flexible about your own goals and willing to try other paths to meet your own higher intentions.

PUBLISHING RESEARCH RESULTS
Publishing is the bread and butter of faculty life and most universities tie performance reviews to publications. One of the greatest challenges in publishing is finding the time to write, polish, and revise the paper or book when there are no specific deadlines for doing so. Be sure to set your own deadlines and goals and set aside some of

your most productive time on a regular basis to accomplish this important task. If you are working with students who will be the primary authors of your publications, assess their writing skills early on and send them to writing classes or workshops if their skills are lacking. This type of investment will better prepare them for any career and will save you substantial time (and frustration) in editing their work.

TEACHING GOALS.

There are many terrific books on teaching so I won't spend too much space on the topic. When I first started as a professor, I went to teaching workshops, read books on the latest teaching methods, and invested substantial time in creating cooperative learning and group activities for my classes. Some of them failed miserably and the students hated them. Eventually I settled on a style that worked for both me and my students, which was a mix of lecturing interspersed with hands-on problem solving. The last time I taught my class, I spent less time than I ever had on the course and got the highest student evaluations ever. Students value stability and high quality materials in a course, something I wasn't able to achieve when I was constantly experimenting and "improving." Moreover, my university's reward system expects quality teaching, but exemplary teaching does not help with tenure, promotions, or raises. I now make incremental improvements to my classes to add some interest and keep them relevant, but save the major experimentation adventures for my research.

For example, I recently added some material from this book to my course to help the students better anticipate and address conflicts that arise in homework teams by collectively defining and focusing on their intentions. For the first time ever, I did not have to intercede to resolve conflicts with any of the homework teams. I also taught the students about fixed and growth mindsets and encouraged them to live in a growth mindset by taking ownership and asking for help if they were struggling in the class, which several students did. The students' grades were higher than ever before (I do not grade on a curve to encourage collaborative learning), but it's too early to know whether that was a trend or a one-semester anomaly.

SERVICE GOALS.

My mentor, Vernon Snoeyink, Emeritus Professor of Environmental Engineering at the University of Illinois, gave me a wonderful piece of advice on service early in my career: *Pick one major service activity and do it well, rather than spreading the same time investment across many minor activities.* I have found his advice to be sound for meeting my needs for making a difference and contributing, as well as workability and feasibility. Don't be afraid to say "no" – I'm sure that no one has ever been denied tenure for turning down a service commitment! Once you take on a service commitment, though, give high priority to making it a success. If it's not worth the investment of your time needed for a successful outcome, don't take it on in the first place!

Leading the WATERS Network was my major service commitment for three years and I consistently turned down any other request for reviewing, organizing conference sessions, or serving on committees that were not closely associated with advancing the WATERS Network. Fortunately, my university was highly supportive and minimized service requests during this period. Prior to the WATERS Network, I focused on an associate editorship and leading a national task committee that created a report on the state of the art in my research area. To the extent possible, choose major service commitments that also advance your highest priority research, teaching, leadership, or personal goals. For example, leading the WATERS Network also helped me to advance my research interests in sensing and cyber-infrastructure for managing complex environmental systems, an area in which I now have several projects. This type of synergy will make the job of balancing progress on your goals much easier.

PERSONAL GOALS.

One of the greatest advantages of being a professor is that our progress is measured by outcomes: publications, students graduated and gainfully employed, awards received, etc. In no way is our performance measured on the number of hours that we spend working or where we work. Take advantage of this wonderful benefit and work where and when you are most productive and creative, rather than when you "should" be at the office. Carve out time in your schedule, whenever it works best, to meet your personal goals. Never neglect your personal goals for long periods, as your productivity will drop, and give high priority to your most critical personal goals, especially taking care of yourself.

It may seem counter-intuitive, but spending time on your personal goals can often lead to improved perform-ance on your professional goals. For example, every Tuesday and Thursday, I usually take a noontime yoga class. That takes almost a two-hour chunk out of the middle of my day, but nonetheless, I've found that I usually get more work done on yoga days because my mind is clearer for focusing in the afternoon and evening.

Chapter Five
C ONCLUSIONS

Real joy comes not from ease or riches or from the praise of men, but from doing something worthwhile.
—Sir Wilfred Grenfell

*I*n this guide, I've proposed a series of steps to bring focus and joy to your life as a professor through: connecting your critical soulful values to your activities and goals, simplifying distractions, and focusing on and balancing the most important activities to meet your needs. Be sure to periodically revisit your needs and goals and update them as needed. Debrief with one or several friends or colleagues on a regular basis to help you make progress.

Over time you will figure out what works best for you to move towards a sustainable life that brings you joy and passion.

Please share what you learn by submitting a comment at http://www.joyfulprofessor.com/contact.php so we can help our faculty community set good examples of work-life integration for our students. Over the years, I have heard many students say that they don't want to become professors because they are afraid they will become like their advisors, overwhelmed and over-worked. It is entirely possible to be a successful faculty member without sacrificing your family, friends, or yourself, but you have to be focused and creative about meeting everyone's most essential needs, and ruthless about saying "no" to distractions. I hope that this guide has provided a structure for doing so, and I welcome your comments and suggestions.

$\mathscr{T}$IPS FOR IDENTIFYING OUTCOMES THAT YOUR INSTITUTION VALUES

*I*f you are just starting out as a professor, it may be difficult to know what is expected for you to get promoted or tenured. Typically there are no hard and fast criteria, but if you ask enough people, you can get a good sense for the boundaries. Talk with your department head or chair, members of your promotion and tenure committee, or senior faculty members and ask them questions like the following:

- On what basis will my performance be judged? Please give specific criteria.

- What would be the minimum number of papers/books above which the number of publications would not be a topic of discussion among those evaluating my case?

- Which journals/publications/conferences in my field are considered the best? If you don't know, how will my evaluators figure that out?

- How will you evaluate my teaching and service?

- Who will make the decision on my promotion or tenure and what will be the process?

- How many reference letters will you request from colleagues in my field and how will you decide who will write them?

Once you know the answers to these questions, you can customize your goals accordingly. For example, getting to know the people who could write your reference letters should be an important goal for your first few years. Service on national committees or workshops or inviting guest lecturers to visit can be a great way to implement that goal.

$\mathcal{R}$ECOMMENDED
RESOURCES

Center for Authentic Leadership
http://www.authenticleadership.com. Life-changing
programs that will help you find your true voice and
communicate more effectively with others, from
your spouse or partner to your colleagues.

Csikszentmihalyi, Mihaly, *Flow: The Psychology of
Optimal Experience*, Harper Perennial, 1991. A
fascinating worldwide study of what makes people
happy.

Dweck, Carol, *Mindset: The New Psychology of Success*,
Ballantine Books, 2007. Presents research on how
dramatically your mindsets towards life challenges
can affect every aspect of your life.

Ferriss, Timothy, *The 4-Hour Work Week: Escape 9-5,
Live Anywhere, and Join the New Rich*, Crown,
2007. This book will open your mind to the creative

possibilities for reducing the number of hours you spend working, as well as the interesting places where you can work.

Insight Meditation Society meditation resources at http://www.dharma.org/ims/ss_meditation_resources.html. Provides useful resources for learning how to meditate and bring more compassion and mindfulness (living in the moment) into your life.

Kabat-Zinn, Jon, *Wherever You Go There You Are: Mindfulness Meditation in Everyday Life*, Hyperion, 1994. A classic book that introduces meditation in a very practical and understandable way.

Ressler, Cali, and Jody Thompson, *Why Work Sucks and How to Fix It: No Schedules, No Meetings, No Joke-- the Simple Change That Can Make Your Job Terrific*, Portfolio Hardcover, 2008. This is a fascinating account of how Best Buy headquarters dramatically improved productivity and employee retention by changing how it does business. It gives interesting ideas for rethinking both your own work style, as well as those of any employees who work for you.

Tolle, Eckhart, *A New Earth: Awakening to Your Life's Purpose*, Penguin, 2008. A useful perspective on how to discover the joy of living life in the moment.

$\mathscr{A}$BOUT THE AUTHOR

$\mathscr{B}$arbara Minsker is Professor of Environmental and Water Resources Systems Engineering in the Department of Civil and Environmental Engineering and National Center for Supercomputing Applications at the University of Illinois Urbana-Champaign. She also serves as Associate Provost Fellow for Sustainability in the Office of the Provost. She began her faculty career at Illinois in 1996 after a four-year stint as an environmental policy consultant in the Washington DC area from 1986-1990, obtaining her Ph.D. at Cornell University from 1990-1995, and serving a one-year stint as a post-doctoral research associate at the University of Vermont. Since joining the faculty, she has won numerous awards for her research, teaching, and service activities.

She has been happily married for 22 years and has two wonderful boys who are 12 and 15 years old as of this writing. In an effort to bring more adventure into her life, she and her son Patrick recently tried out canyoneering in Utah, a truly joyful undertaking!